# TAUNTON
## THROUGH TIME
Simon Haines

AMBERLEY PUBLISHING

**The Great Hall, Taunton Castle, *c.* 1905**
An interior picture-postcard view of how Taunton's museum looked in the first years of the twentieth century.

First published 2013

Amberley Publishing
The Hill, Stroud, Gloucestershire, GL5 4EP
www.amberley-books.com

Copyright © Simon Haines, 2013

The right of Simon Haines to be identified as the
Author of this work has been asserted in accordance with
the Copyrights, Designs and Patents Act 1988.

ISBN  978 1 4456 1644 5 (print)
ISBN  978 1 4456 1663 6 (ebook)

British Library Cataloguing in Publication Data.
A catalogue record for this book is available from the
British Library.

Typesetting by Amberley Publishing.
Printed in Great Britain.

# Introduction

Almost 200 images in this book about Taunton, the county town of Somerset, have been paired together to allow the reader to compare early twentieth-century views of the town with photographs taken of Taunton as it appears today. This has resulted in most cases in a gap of at least 100 years between the two pictures presented on each page.

The overall aim of this work is to present the viewer with as close a corresponding view as possible, and in most cases my present-day photographs have been taken from a very similar viewpoint to that of the photographer of the original photograph. On occasion, due to changes in road traffic, the relocation and rebuilding of buildings and streets, or concerns over privacy, this has not been possible. Similarly, changes in camera and lens technology over the intervening period have meant that even if the original photographer had stood on exactly the same spot as I had, the image may still appear to be slightly different. Nonetheless, despite the changes that have taken place in Taunton and the gap in time between the images presented, many pairings remain strikingly alike.

The majority of early images have been taken from old picture postcards the author has collected over the last ten years or so, chiefly at antique markets and via online purchases. It is fair to state that in the years prior to the First World War postcards were an extremely common and popular way of communicating with friends and family. Indeed, such is the number of postcards still in existence, it would appear that writing and posting a postcard was quite as usual 100 years past as sending an email or SMS text message is today. Thankfully, for the purposes of this work and history many thousands of these local picture postcards have survived the passing of years in the drawers and albums of so many collectors. Other than the sourcing of historic images through old postcards, a smaller number of the archive pictures contained within the pages of this book have been obtained by reprinting from old glass negatives and original private photographs in the author's archive.

The dating of original images can never be an exact science, unless as was the case in a handful of the images used the specific date was recorded. Otherwise dates have been taken from postmarks recorded on the reverse of the postcards themselves, historical research into the material changes occurring in Taunton, and through close examination of things like the clothing worn by people pictured or motor vehicles present. As a result, the majority of dates cited are probably accurate within plus or minus five years. The photographs of present-day Taunton included were all taken between the months of January and May 2013.

The photographs in this pictorial tour of past and present Taunton have been presented in an order that loosely approximates a walk around the centre of Taunton, beginning close to the railway station and ending up with visits to some of the larger and most striking of the town's many churches.

## St Andrew's Church and Room, Greenway Avenue, *c.* 1910

We begin this pictorial past and present tour of the town at the church, built in 1881 to serve the rapidly expanding area around the newly arrived Great Western Railway. Indeed, such were the church's ties to the railway it became known as the Railway Parish. Today, the church still holds weekly services and runs a well-attended Sunday school. The Room, shown to the left of the picture, now provides accommodation for 'single professionals'.

**Tracked Vehicle, Station Approach, Station Road, *c.* 1915**
A petrol engine-driven Holt tractor heading towards the station. These tracked vehicles were used during the First World War to move heavy guns on the Western Front. In the background, the now long-demolished railway engine sheds and large detached railway worker's house can be seen. If you look carefully, a tram can be seen passing along Station Road in the distance.

**Station Road, c. 1904**

An electric tram, heading from the station towards the town centre and its terminus at the bottom of East Reach. The building between what was then the Royal Mail stores and the Crown & Sceptre Hotel housed a grocery shop, which, as you will notice in our present-day view, is no longer there. The building was demolished in 1923 to make way for Priory Bridge Road.

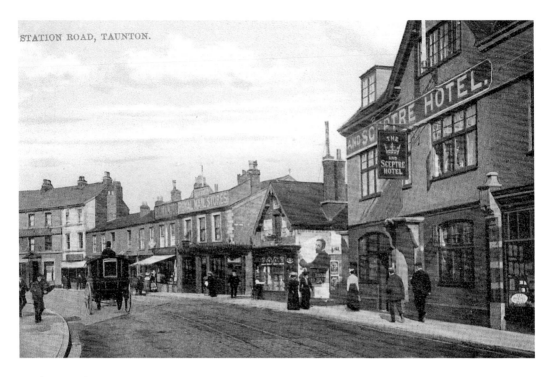

STATION ROAD, TAUNTON.

**Station Road, *c.* 1910**
Another look at the Crown & Sceptre Hotel, Tom Male's grocery, and the Royal Mail stores, at what was then the narrow entrance from Station Road to Canal Road. Note the use of the side of the grocer's to display posters advertising upcoming events and products.

**Station Road, *c.* 1911**
Westlake's Cycle Depot and now long-disappeared front gardens can be seen in this old picture-postcard view of Station Road, between Belverdere Road and Albemarle Road. Note the passing loop and rather elaborate stanchions of the tram system.

**Bridge Street, *c.* 1906**
A wonderfully animated photograph of Bridge Street looking towards the town centre. On the left is the Telegraph Inn. In the distance is the top of the tower of St Mary's church.

**Bridge Street, *c.* 1909**

Shops including Baker's Stationary Stores and, in the distance, the Lyceum Cinema (later the Classic), located at the junction of Bridge Street, Station Road and Staplegrove Road. The cinema building was demolished in the late 1990s and was replaced by housing association flats.

Bridge Street, *c.* 1905
Horse-drawn carts, a handcart, tram, and the interesting Winter & Son store, which according to the display advertisement offered everything from linoleum to antiques. Opposite is a billboard advertising Goodland & Sons, merchants who sold coal, coke, salt, firewood and related items in and around Taunton for many years.

**The Bridge, *c.* 1912**

A photograph taken from the middle of the bridge over the River Tone looking in the direction of North Street. Meetam & Lewis Sporting Outfitters can be seen on the left. The Singer Sewing Machine shop is on the right-hand side. Other than the Debenhams department store building and an increase in road traffic, the scene looks much the same today.

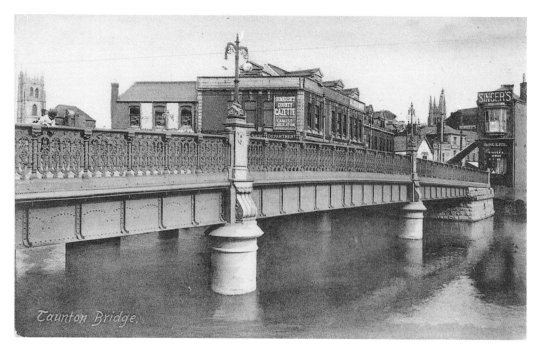

**Taunton Bridge, *c.* 1910**
The ornate and attractive town centre bridge over the River Tone. The towers of both St James's church and St Mary's church are visible in this picture-postcard view. The bridge itself was built in 1894 and replaced a previous stone-built bridge.

**Deller's Café, Bridge Street, *c.* 1923**
The rather impressive Deller's Café and the town bridge. Interior images of Deller's Café between the wars testify to the upmarket, grand appearance and standing of what was by all accounts a popular meeting place for Tauntonians with money to spend. Early motor cars and handcarts compete for space on the road.

**The Bridge, c. 1905**
An earlier picture-postcard view of the Tone Bridge, showing the older industrial building, which prior to its demolition and the building of Deller's Café housed Henry Corners & Company's woollen manufacturer's and Trood's Potato Warehouse.

**North Street, c. 1905**
Here we are moving towards the very centre of the town and into Bridge Street. On the right of the picture is Chapman's department store, which has been a Debenhams since the early 1970s. Behind the tram and in the distance the Market House can be seen.

### North Street, c. 1911

A twenty-four-seater electric tram, seen here in a postcard sent to an address in the nearby town of Wiveliscombe and postmarked 1911. The same rather splendid clock is still be seen on the post office, but in the 2013 photograph it is obscured by the foliage of the comparatively recently planted trees.

**North Street and Post Office, *c.* 1920**
Horses and carts, handcarts, cyclists, and an increasing number of motor cars compete for space around the main post office, which first opened its doors in 1911. Apart from the addition of cycle lanes and the replacement of several smaller shops with large chain stores, the bustling atmosphere and general look remains remarkably similar today.

*North Street, c. 1940*
Twenty years later, the horses and carts have disappeared to be replaced by motor vehicles of various types, and parking appears to have begun to cause problems. Note the addition of the large British Home Stores building. A look at the recent photograph might leave one the false impression that the centre is relatively traffic-free, which, of course, it isn't.

Castle Hotel

**The Castle Hotel and Kingslake Memorial, *c.* 1910**
No traffic, but a rather motley collection of onlookers are seen here outside the North Street frontage of the Castle Hotel and beside the memorial to the Kingslake family, which was commonly referred to as the Market Cross. The memorial itself was demolished in the early 1930s. The splendid grey stone Burtons building shown in the picture below was completed in 1929.

**Castle Gateway, c. 1905**
The gateway of Clarke's Hotel, which later joined with the Castle Hotel, as seen here from North Street. The Winchester Hotel can be seen in the distance through the arch. Note the addition of the extra storey to the gateway in the recent photograph.

**Parade and Market Cross, *c.* 1910**
Horse-drawn hansom cabs can be seen here, parked waiting for fares at the Parade – a triangular island in the centre of the town. Note the absence of the arcades on the Market House in the present-day photograph. These arches were removed in around 1930 to make way for the ever-increasing numbers of motor vehicles.

The Town Hall and Parade, *c.* 1955
A later view of what was the Town Hall and the Parade area dating back to the 1950s. As recorded in the picture below, the town centre has been subject to much pedestrianisation and arguably improvement in recent times.

**North Street and the Parade, *c.* 1940**
An old picture postcard showing the view from the Market House looking down North Street towards the Bridge Street area. The message on the reverse refers to a romantic first meeting on the Parade between the sender of the postcard and the recipient, who it seems lived in the nearby town of Ilminster!

**The Market, *c.* 1910**
In this vintage photograph we have a close-up view of the market, which was held on the Parade up until the 1930s. The weekly farmers' market is now held every Thursday a few hundred metres away in the High Street.

St. Mary's Church and Hammet Street, Taunton. ✕ *This is the market place*

**St Mary's Church and Hammett Street, *c.* 1905**
The view looking down Hammett Street from the Parade towards the 50-metre-high tower of St Mary Magdalene Church. When comparing the past and present shots of the same spot one will note the appearance of a monument cross in the latter. As will be explained in later pages, the Burmese Cross has moved from its original position.

**Hammet Street, _c._ 1911**

A wonderful array of Tauntonians and their hats at an unknown parade – possibly connected with the Coronation of King George V in 1911 – up Hammett Street. The street itself was built at the end of the nineteenth century and is named after the Member of Parliament at the time, Sir Benjamin Hammett.

### Fore Street, c. 1933

Here we have an old picture postcard of the roundabout that once stood at the bottom of the High Street. Close inspection of the earlier image reveals a policeman standing watch over traffic, signage warning motorists to keep left, and a signpost detailing miles to various distances – Barnstaple 50, Minehead 24, Honiton 17, Sidmouth 28. This particular area of the town is now largely pedestrianised.

**Fore Street, *c.* 1910**

A super, very detailed image of some of the oldest buildings in Taunton. In the earlier image the shops included the Devon and Somerset Stores, which offered everything from tea to wicker baskets, and the West Somerset Stores, purveyors of Anglo-Bavarian ales and stout. The building housing the Devon and Somerset Stores was regrettably demolished in the late 1960s. A similarly styled building is now home to a Clarks shoe store.

## Fore Street, c. 1950

A later traffic-filled view of the same part of the town centre. This spot today has lost all its road traffic and is home to a number of coffee shops and cafés, various food stalls and, at weekends, the odd busker or two. It is a fine spot to just sit and people watch.

Taunton, Fore Street, Old House (A.D. 1578)

**Old House, Fore Street, c. 1910**
This building, dating back to at least 1578, is believed to be Taunton's oldest building still in existence. In this earlier picture it houses Halliday Antiques. Today, it is home to a Café Nero coffee shop.

## Interior of Tudor House, Fore Street, c. 1909

Here we have interior views of what has been described as the Banqueting Hall of Ye Olde Tudor House past and present. The building, parts of which are said to date back to the fourteenth century, was in past times the town house of the Portman family.

Banqueting Hall.

YE OLDE TUDOR HOUSE, 15 Fore St., TAUNTON.
Containing Showrooms and Galleries replete with interesting examples of
Old World Furniture, China, &c. for sale at strictly commercial prices.
F. G. HALLIDAY (1909) Ltd., Antique Dealers.
Ye Odds & Ye Ends, Taunton. Minehead, Eton, Banbury & Porlock.
Specialities : Week-End Cottages furnished throughout.   Collections formed and augmented.

**A Parade on the Parade, c. 1911**

Policemen, the Major, and numerous local dignitaries are pictured during what was likely the parade honouring the Coronation of King George V in 1911. Note the white gloves and top hats. These pictures were taken looking in the direction of the original location of the Burmese Cross and the north side of Fore Street where it meets with East Street.

Fore Street and Burmese Memorial, *c.* 1910

A fifty-one-seater, double-decker, open-top electric tram pictured near the Burmese memorial. The cross dates back to 1889 and was erected to commemorate local men killed in the Burma campaign of 1862.

**Fore Street, *c.* 1911**
A view looking towards the Market House with the now demolished arcade arches clearly visible.
Marshalsea's Garage is to the left of the picture. The Clements & Brown store is to the right.

Fore Street, *c.* 1911
Early motor cars, a single-decker tram, cyclists and pedestrians are pictured in this old photograph taken from Fore Street in the direction of East Street.

**North Street and Burma Cross, *c.* 1909**
Here one can compare the original positioning of the Burma Cross with its current location in the centre of the Parade. Note also the intricate electrical cables and supporting posts of the tram system.

London Hotel. Taunton.
Proprietor, E. H. Claridge.
Head-Quarters of the Automobile Club.
'Phone. 134.

**Automobile Club Meeting at Claridge's London Hotel, East Street, 1904**
A meeting of the Somerset Automobile Club and a group of French motorists gathered outside the headquarters of the club, the then Claridge's London Hotel. Later this became the County Hotel, and the building is now divided between a Waterstones bookshop and a Marks & Spencer department store.

**East Street, c. 1920**
A look through the entrance of the County Hotel down East Street towards East Reach. The hotel may have disappeared but the view today is remarkably similar.

**East Street, c. 1910**

This extremely busy picture-postcard view really captures the atmosphere of pre-First World War Taunton. Close inspection of the original image reveals a pony and trap, horse and carriages, street tram, handcart, and a large number of Tauntonians going about their everyday business, some of whom are also observing the photographer. On the left two women can be seen looking at the display of photographs in the window of a photographer's studio. Everybody present appears to be wearing either a cap or hat.

East Street, Taunton

### East Street, c. 1912
Another busy early twentieth-century Taunton street scene, including the Brooks Dye Works on the left and a rather overloaded horse and cart. The area today is home to several fast-food establishments, the Perkin Warbeck public house, and several busy shops including a sports store, an optician's, and a large clothing store.

**East Street, c. 1910**
A picture-postcard view of the Old Council House building, which at various times accommodated the Local Board of Health and the offices of the Taunton Corporation. Today, the building is vacant and the agents are advertising the premises for use as a restaurant or bar.

Taunton, Old Almshouses.

Old Almshouses, East Street, *c.* 1910

A real step back in time here with a postman taking a rest from his delivery to observe the photographer and chat with another bystander. Also visible in the vintage image are the Pope's Almshouses, Grey's Almshouses, two small shops, and a public water pump. Pope's Almshouses, on the left of the picture, were founded in the sixteenth century, and demolished in the 1930s to make room for Dunn's Motor Company.

East Street, *c.* 1905

The junction of East Street, East Reach and Silver Street. To the left is a granite drinking fountain, which was moved from this location to Vivary Park not long after this photograph was taken. One of many CCTV cameras now stands in a spot not too far from where the fountain once stood.

Tracked Vehicle and Howitzer Gun, East Reach, *c.* 1914

In this photograph, a tracked vehicle can be seen pulling a Howitzer gun past Paul's pawnbroker's in the first year of the First World War. Today the building houses the rather good Cornerstone Café. Unfortunately, this location is where pedestrian footfall declines drastically, and as a result many businesses appear to find it difficult to survive very long.

East Reach, *c.* 1910

Looking down East Reach hill with a street tram in the distance. The Racehorse Inn is on the left.

**East Reach Hill, _c._ 1909**
The Naval & Military Inn is centre stage in this picture-postcard view. The pub itself closed down several years ago but still bears the original signage. Below, we see yet another recently placed CCTV camera.

East Reach, *c.* 1909
In this view of the bottom end of the street we can see the Taunton and Somerset Hospital and Nursing Institute on the right.

**East Reach, c. 1906**
Another picture postcard illustrating the hospital and nursing institute. The hospital opened in 1812 and the institute in 1888. Both buildings now serve different purposes.

**East Reach, *c.* 1905**
This image was taken from the furthest point down East Reach hill to feature in this collection. As in the previous two pictures the hospital and institute feature prominently.

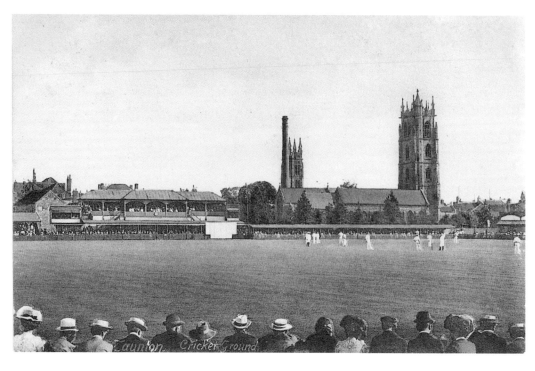

Cricket Ground, *c.* 1905
The home ground of Somerset County Cricket Club. The towers of St Mary's church and St James's church are clearly visible in both the past and present images.

Old Catholic Church       Priory, Taunton

### Old Catholic Church Priory, *c.* 1905

This is one of the only surviving buildings from the medieval period in the town. This old postcard, depicting a semi-derelict former Catholic church, is now the home of the County Cricket Museum.

**Fore Street, c. 1939**

This postcard finds us back in the centre of the town again. Prominent are the relatively newly created traffic roundabout and arcade-less Market House building. This part of the town is now a much more pedestrian-friendly area.

Corporation Street, Showing Municipal Buildings, *c. 1910*
Contrasting views of the same part of the centre of Taunton. Other than the Municipal Buildings in the distance, the Old Angel public house and Prudential Assurance building feature.

**Fore Street, from Corporation Street, *c.* 1910**
The view from the Municipal Buildings back towards the Market House. The arcade arches of the Market House are clearly visible in the earlier image.

## The Municipal Buildings, *c.* 1910

The Municipal Buildings were originally built in the early sixteenth century as Taunton Grammar School by Bishop Richard Fox. The property was acquired by the town council in 1887 for municipal use and is now largely used by the Major and as a wedding venue. As can be seen in the recent photograph, the town's main taxi rank and the bus stop for the park and ride bus service are situated in front of the building.

**The Public Library, *c.* 1907**
Opposite the Municipal Buildings is the Free Library building. The library opened at the end of
1904, but was replaced several years later when a new library was created in the space under the
multi-storey car park. The old library is now home to the Pitcher & Piano public house.

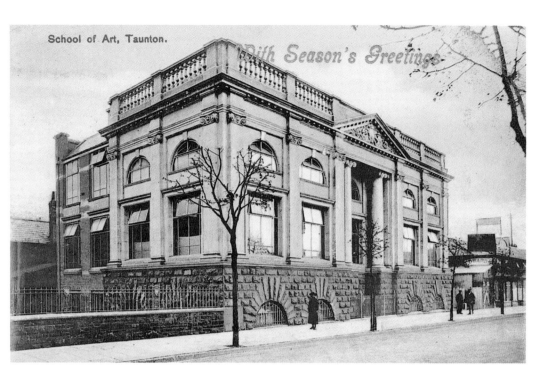

School of Art, Taunton.

With Season's Greetings

## School of Art Building, *c.* 1909

Probably one of Taunton's better buildings, the School of Art opened just two years before this postcard was posted by a student studying there to his grandparents in Wells. Today the building accommodates a rather swanky restaurant and café.

Technical Institute, *c.* 1905
Opened in 1900 as the Scientific and Technical Institute for Taunton, this is now home to the Apple & Parrot public house.

**Castle Green, c. 1930**

A general view of Castle Green, looking across to what was the main car park for the town, and on to the castle and Castle Hotel. This part of the town has recently been converted into a pedestrian-friendly area, with the car park grassed over and open areas created.

TAUNTON CASTLE

Taunton Castle, *c.* 1904
An old picture postcard of the Norman castle as it looked at the very beginning of the twentieth century. The building now houses the County Museum and has been designated a Grade I listed building by English Heritage.

Norman Keep · Taunton Castle

*This will match the other one. Am very pleased to hear that you are amongst the Collectors of P. Post Cards. Yours Sincerely.*

Stengel & Co., London E. C. 39 Redcross Street 16428

**Norman Keep, c. 1904**
The keep and rear of the castle. In the recent photograph two people can be seen attempting to draw a sword from a stone in the manner of the King Arthur legend!

**Castle Gateway, c. 1902**
The entrance to the castle, now the gateway to the quite wonderful and recently refurbished Museum of Somerset.

Courtyard, Taunton Castle

**Courtyard, Taunton Castle, *c.* 1910**
Once through the gateway visitors come into the castle courtyard. The recent shot shows a rather nice café, a part of what has recently been done to upgrade the museum.

**The Winchester Hotel, c. 1920**
An old photograph of the Winchester Hotel and the sheep pens, part of what was the town's market in Castle Green.

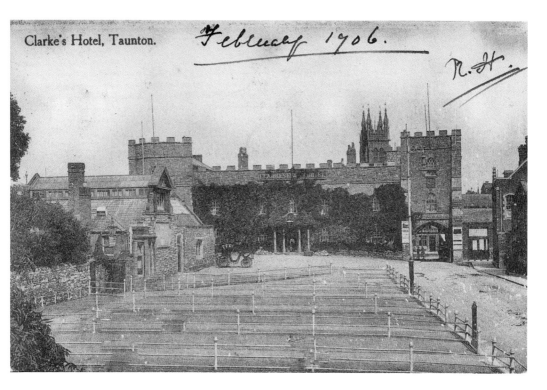

Clarke's Hotel, Taunton.    *February 1906.*    R.H.

**Clarke's Hotel, c. 1906**

A building that was originally built in the style of a twelfth-century Norman fortress as a private residence in 1815 – it was converted to a hotel in the 1830s. In this picture-postcard view, the sheep pens of the town's animal market can clearly be seen in front of a two-storey Clarke's Hotel. A third storey was added in the early 1920s, and a fourth added in 1965. The building today operates as the four-star Castle Hotel, and is Grade II listed.

**Castle Hotel, c. 1930**

The same building not long after the third floor had been added. In the recent image, wisteria can be seen growing over much of the walls of the building, disguising and adding to the generally held belief that the building has always been of the same height.

Tangier Bridge, *c.* 1905
The footbridge over Tone Mill Stream. In times past Tangier Brewery was based in the buildings behind the bridge.

**Corporation Street, c. 1939**
The Four Alls Hotel and Somerset Motors as seen from the top end of the street. Today the Four Alls is an Indian restaurant, and the Somerset Motors buildings were demolished to provide office space for HMRC.

**County Hall, _c._ 1939**
County Hall, the Home of Somerset County Council, with St John's church in the distance. Only the Debenhams offices, built during the 1960s, have changed the look of this part of Taunton.

Park Street, Taunton.

**Park Street, *c.* 1905**

Here we have an extremely quiet-looking street scene, with its Victorian housing and St John's church partially obscured by trees. Although the buildings remain largely unchanged, Park Street is now fairly difficult to photograph, due to the ever-present and surprisingly fast-moving traffic.

SHIRE HALL, TAUNTON. 7923

**Shire Hall, *c.* 1920**
The Victorian Gothic Shire Hall was built in the 1850s and is home to the Crown Court.

**The Crescent, c. 1905**

A view of the Masonic Hall and the Georgian buildings of the Crescent from the Upper High Street end looking towards Corporation Street. The Masonic Hall was built as a Roman Catholic church in 1812, and is a Grade II listed building.

**High Street, *c.* 1920**

This superb old picture postcard features a simply splendid array of motor vehicles, and a lady cyclist is pictured cycling right in the centre of the street. As can be seen in the present-day photograph, the High Street has been pedestrianised and is an altogether different sort of place.

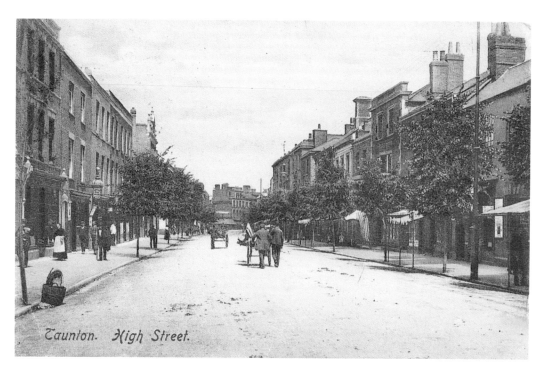

High Street, c. 1905
The same street fifteen years earlier. Here handcarts take the place of motor cars.

**High Street, c. 1909**
The top end of the High Street looking down towards Fore Street in the far distance. Note the fairly recently planted trees lining the pavements in the earlier image.

HIGH STREET - TAUNTON

**High Street, c. 1905**
Another picture-postcard view of the very end of the High Street just where it meets Upper High Street. Behind the photographer would have been the gates to Vivary Park, as seen in the later image.

### The Park Gates, *c.* 1905

Here we have photographs of the gates of the wonderful green space that is Vivary Park. The gates were erected shortly after the purchase of the land from a local family by the town in the early 1890s. The name Vivary is derived from the word vivaria (fish ponds), some of which were formerly located on the site.

Fountain in Vivary Park, *c.* 1907

The Diamond Jubilee memorial fountain was built to commemorate the life and reign of Queen Victoria. It is still attracting the attention of visitors, young and old, more than 100 years later.

**Feeding Swans in Vivary Park, c. 1910**
Tauntonian folk gathered for the photographer and to feed the swans on the artificial stream, which runs through the park. Today the majority of the birds on the stream are seagulls rather than swans or ducks.

Taunton    Feeding the Ducks, Vivary Park

The Wrench Series No. 6615

**Feeding the Ducks, Vivary Park, *c.* 1905**
Another look at the park. In the background we can see the bandstand, the central focus of many events in the park.

**The War Memorial, Vivary Park, *c.* 1922**
The Portland stone and Cornish granite monument to almost 500 soldiers from Taunton who were killed in the First World War.

The Barracks, *c. 1910*

A view of Jellalabad Barracks from Vivary Park. The barracks, built in 1880 and home to the Somerset Light Infantry for many years, were named after a conflict in the first Afghan War of 1842. The Army have long since departed the building and it has now been converted into flats.

**Elm Grove, *c.* 1902**
A quiet, leafy, residential street not far from the busy Station Road.

**French Weir, c. 1908**

At the beginning of the twentieth century, this location on the River Tone was a popular spot for bathing and boating, and even had its own bathing huts. Today, very few people would want to swim in the river here, but it remains a well-visited part of Taunton, especially by parents and young children using the playground, and dog walkers. The horse chestnut trees visible in both pictures were planted in 1898.

**Roughmoor, c. 1905**
The River Tone where it flows from the French Weir heading out towards Bishops Hull is known as Roughmoor. It remains a fairly popular spot for walkers and anglers.

**Taunton School, c. 1910**

Here we have two images of cricket being played in the grounds of the private, independent Taunton School. The school was formerly known as the Independent College, with the main buildings being built in 1870.

**Sherford, c. 1905**
The picturesque bridge over Sherford Stream shown on an old picture postcard sent from Taunton to Posen in Germany.

**St George's Church and Rectory,** *c.* **1910**
Completed and dedicated to St George in 1860, this is the larger and most splendid of the two
Roman Catholic churches in Taunton.

**St James's Church, *c.* 1911**
The Church of St James was built in the early fourteenth century on the site of an earlier tenth-century church. The 34-metre-high tower dates back to the 1870s, and forms a familiar backdrop to the Somerset County Cricket Ground.

**The Church, Bishops Hull, *c.* 1907**
Dedicated to St Peter and St Paul, this church on the outskirts of the town dates back in part to the fourteenth century.

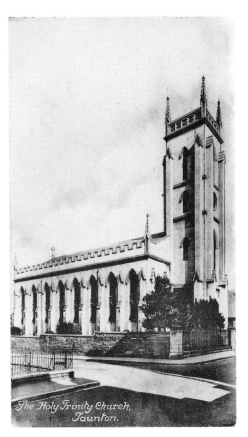

**Trinity Church, c. 1910**
Built in 1842, with an impressive 30-metre-high tower and a ring of six bells, the white lias clad Holy Trinity Church is probably Taunton's only church to describe itself as Anglo-Catholic.

**St John's Church, *c.* 1905**
Work on this beautiful church began in 1858 and the church was dedicated to St John the Evangelist in 1863.

ST. MARY'S CHURCH, TAUNTON.    4398

**St Mary's Church, c. 1903**

The Church of St Mary Magdalene was completed in 1508. Built in Early Tudor Perpendicular Gothic style, it is in the opinion of many the most impressive building in Taunton. It is of sandstone construction and features a painted interior, a truly beautiful 50-metre-high tower with twelve bells and a noteworthy clock mechanism. St Mary's has been designated a Grade I listed building by English Heritage.

Taunton, Batts Park Bridge.

**Batt's Park Bridge,** *c.* **1906**
Sometimes known as the Roman bridge, this ancient stone-built bridge looks much the same more than 100 years after the earlier postcard was produced.